NATURE DETECTIVES

A walk on the beach

Jo Waters

Heinemann
LIBRARY

Little Nippers

H **www.heinemann.co.uk/library**
Visit our website to find out more information about **Heinemann Library** books.

To order:
☎ Phone 44 (0) 1865 888066
▤ Send a fax to 44 (0) 1865 314091
▢ Visit the Heinemann Bookshop at www.heinemann.co.uk/library to browse our catalogue and order online.

First published in Great Britain by Heinemann Library, Halley Court, Jordan Hill, Oxford OX2 8EJ, part of Harcourt Education. Heinemann is a registered trademark of Harcourt Education Ltd.

Editorial: Kathy Peltan and Clare Lewis
Design: Jo Hinton-Malivoire and
   Tinstar Design Ltd (www.tinstar.co.uk)
Picture Research: Maria Joannou and Rebecca Sodergren
Production: Camilla Smith

Originated by Dot Gradations Ltd.
Printed and bound in China by South China Printing Company

10-digit ISBN 0 431 17160 2
13-digit ISBN 978 0 431 17160 9
10 09 08 07 06
10 9 8 7 6 5 4 3 2 1

British Library Cataloguing in Publication Data
Waters, Jo
578.7'699
Nature Detectives: A Walk on the Beach
A full catalogue record for this book is available from the British Library.

Acknowledgements
The Publishers would like to thank the following for permission to reproduce photographs:
Alamy Images/colinspics p. 19; Ardea/Bob Gibbons p. 12; Ardea/Richard Vaughan p.21; Corbis p. 10; FLPA/Frans Lanting/Minden Pictures p. 13; FLPA/Hugh Clark p16; Harcourt Education/Malcolm Harris pp. 4, 5, 6, 7, 8, 17, 18, 22, 23; Getty Images/Photodisc pp. 10, 11; NHPA/James Carmichael Jr p. 14; NHPA/Mike Lane p. 20; Photolibrary p. 15.

Cover photograph reproduced with permission of Corbis/Craig Tuttle.

Our thanks to Annie Davy and Michael Scott for their assistance in the preparation of this book.

Every effort has been made to contact copyright holders of any material reproduced in this book. Any omissions will be rectified in subsequent printings if notice is given to the Publishers.

Contents

By the sea

Where are we?
We are at the beach!

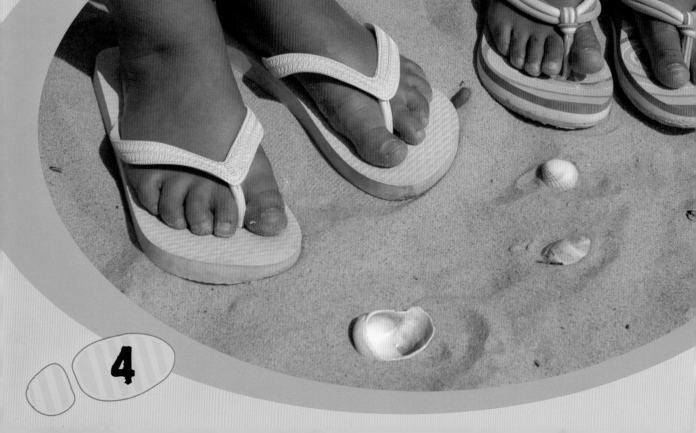

The waves make a swishing sound.

Sandy beach

The beach is sandy. Dry sand is soft and gritty.

6

Wet sand is great for building sandcastles.

Pebbles

Pebbles can be rough and smooth, little and big.

8

And all sorts of colours!

Beachcombing

You can find lots of other treasures too.

Sea shells

Some shells are snail-shaped.

Some shells look like wings.

13

Who is hiding?

Who lives in this shell?

A hermit
crab. Hello!

Seaweed

Can you find some seaweed?

It feels slimy and slippery.

In the water

The water tickles our toes.

Look closer at
the tiny fish.

Look up high

Seagulls fly high in the sky.

20

They screech
and squawk.

Time to go home

Goodbye sea.

We brush the sand off our feet.
We're leaving.

23

Index

Notes for adults

This series encourages children to explore their environment to gain knowledge and understanding of the things they can see, smell, hear, taste, and feel. The following Early Learning Goals are relevant to the series:

• use the senses to explore and learn about the world around them
• investigate objects and materials by using all of their senses as appropriate
• find out about living things, objects and events they observe
• observe and identify features in the place they live and the natural world
• find out about their environment, and talk about those features they like and dislike.

The following additional information may be of interest

Exploring the natural world at an early age can help promote awareness of the environment and general understanding of life processes. Discussing the seasons with children can be a good way of helping them understand the concepts of time, patterns and change. Identifying features that people share with insects and animals can promote understanding of similarities.

Follow-up activities

• Encourage children to think and talk about why people should take care of the environment and not damage plants or harm animals.
• Ask children to think about the sounds they might hear at the beach.
• Encourage children to use all their senses to feel, look at, and describe a pebble. Invite comments about all aspects of pebbles, including colour, texture, smell, sound.

24